MW01701861

Dear
Gracie

May your dreams
be used to change
the world
and become a world changer

Pray and believe for HANA

Sally J. Messerrett

HANA

CROSSES THE FREEDOM BRIDGE

a story of how Korea becomes ONE

하나

Sally Jo Messersmith

Illustrated By Krystyna Speaks

Author's Notes

the story behind the story

This is a story of hope, a prayer for peace, for the children of Korea, a country divided by war years ago.

The Korean Conflict began in June of 1950 and lasted until July 1953, ending with the Korean Armistice Agreement. Part of the resolution was to create the Demilitarized Zone (DMZ) at the 38th parallel.

The DMZ is 155 miles long and is approximately 2 & 1/2 miles wide, dividing North Korea and South Korea. The area is beautiful; however, we refer to it as *THE UGLIEST PLACE IN THE WORLD* because for the past 70 years it has separated families, friends, and continues to divide the Korean people.

North Korea is referred to as *THE PLACE WHERE DREAMS DIE* in this allegory because its government has actively worked to put out the dreams, ideas and even hopes of its own people. The citizens of North Korea are not allowed to learn about Jesus, talk about freedom, or learn how to live a better life without serious consequences, even if they have not committed any real crime.

North Korea punishes any citizen with different ideas in terrible ways:

- Imprisoning whole families, including children, in labor camps called "Gulags."
- Starving their citizens to feed the military.
- Killing anyone who openly disagrees with them or tries to escape.

Many North Koreans have secretly escaped from their own country in search of food, safety, and freedom. These people are called defectors. When they escape, they have to make their way through China (many live in China for years in hiding) before reaching South Korea.

South Korea is a country where families live and work freely. In this story, it is called THE PLACE OF FREEDOM. South Korea has welcomed 30,000 North Korean defectors as citizens without hesitation, allowing them to have ideas, hopes, dreams and freedom.

North Korean defectors living in South Korea miss their families and are concerned for their safety. They want their fellow North Koreans to know about the freedom they have discovered in South Korea. Many of them have also become Christians, and they want to share their new-found faith with the oppressed people of their native land, just a few short miles away.

One of the unique ways that South Koreans are able to discreetly spread faith and hope to isolated North Koreans is by sending high tech balloons across the DMZ in the middle of the night. They attach Bibles and messages of hope and freedom to these balloons, praying that they will be found by the needy citizens.

Many Korean Christians believe that LOVE is the only thing that will heal their broken nation. They believe that the people of Korea (not the governments) will have to be the ones to take a stand, ultimately bringing the two nations together as one.

The Freedom Bridge is located inside of the DMZ next to Imjingak Village in South Korea. It crosses near the Imijin River, reaching towards North Korea. Though the bridge is blocked, preventing anyone from crossing, it stands as a visual message of hope: Hope that one day The Freedom Bridge will be crossed by North Koreans and South Koreans; hope that one day the DMZ separating the two countries will no longer exist; hope that one day the divided country will become ONE Korea; hope that one day Korea will become HANA.

This story is not true yet, but perhaps, one day it will be. Then the children may really live in peace and harmony.

An Invitation to all children to Pray:

Our hope is that this story will inspire the free children of the world to pray for the freedom and safety of the people, especially the children, of North Korea. Pray that they'll continue to fight for their own freedom.

Remember, one child matters. One hope, one dream, and one prayer of even one child can change the world. YOU can change the world with LOVE.

The Freedom Bridge crosses over
THE UGLIEST PLACE IN THE WORLD.
Strangely, it is a place of beauty. As far as the eye can see are trees that stretch to the sky, rolling hills with exotic animals roaming them, and streams gently meandering in and out of secret places. Why then is this place called
THE UGLIEST PLACE IN THE WORLD?

It is ugly
because it was
built to separate.
It separates friends,
it separates family,
it separates husbands and wives,
and if possible,
The Creator from His children.

The Freedom Bridge glistens in the sunlight, longingly waiting to be crossed, but it is blocked off from the people.

Children are gathering
at the entrance of
the bridge, in the land called
THE PLACE OF FREEDOM.
How can this day own a bluer sky?
Can the sun shine with more brilliance?
Maybe the excitement in the faces of the
children reflects into the heavens?

Soon time will be handed over to them, and they will release their dreams. Their dreams will be carried to *THE PLACE WHERE DREAMS DIE*, on the other side of *THE UGLIEST PLACE IN THE WORLD*. They are hopeful and expectant that their dreams will not be extinguished.

Even though they are young, what they have in their hands is powerful. Powerful like a revolution:
WORDS.
The words are written
on dream filled balloons:
JOY,
LIFE,
PEACE,
FREEDOM,
HOPE,
and
LOVE.
The wind is
strong this day,
and blowing in a
northerly direction.
The wind knows it has
an important mission.
To deliver the words to:
THE PLACE WHERE DREAMS DIE.

A little girl named Sung has a balloon like all the other children. In her balloon she places a special seed that came from a flower that she found on top of a mountain. She chose to send this special seed because the flower reminds her of a balloon filled with free air. The petals unite at the top and cannot fall apart, like her dream: HANA.

HANA.
A word
so simple,
yet the dream
behind
it is powerful.
In her
language,
HANA means
ONE.
In her heart,
HANA means
that
THE PLACE WHERE DREAMS DIE
will be transformed by LOVE and
will unite with THE PLACE OF FREEDOM.

This is an impossible dream, but even still, she writes the word HANA in bold letters on her balloon. With her balloon filled with an impossible dream in her hand, she whispers the prayer of HANA to Jesus, the Creator, who can make ALL things possible.

The Children say a prayer for all of the balloons.
Then a signal is given for everyone to release their dream filled balloons to be carried to *THE PLACE WHERE DREAMS DIE.*

Dreams must be let go. Dreams must be shared with others. Dreams can be more real than what we see, more real than what is called reality. The fact is, HOPE starts with a DREAM!

The Freedom Bridge shows the path over
THE UGLIEST PLACE IN THE WORLD
for all of the balloons to follow. The wind picks
up Sung's balloon like all the other balloons...

...however, at an angelic speed,
the wind carries Sung's balloon higher.
And along with all the others, it travels
over *THE UGLIEST PLACE IN THE WORLD*
into *THE PLACE WHERE DREAMS DIE.*

All of the other balloons land along their journey and deliver their important dreams:

JOY,
PEACE,
FREEDOM,
HOPE,
and
LOVE.

However,
the HANA
balloon
continues
on into the
deepest,
darkest
part of
THE PLACE WHERE DREAMS DIE.

The HANA balloon finally lands and pops on the ground, releasing the seed which is slowly buried into the hardened soil. It dies there, as all seeds do. Dreams do the same sometimes - they die. They are like this seed and seem to be gone forever.

But they are not dead.
Someday they will begin to grow again.

Thousands upon thousands of dreams,
spoken and unspoken, are buried
in this hardened soil.
These dreams are spoken in prayers,
released, buried and then
dreamed again.

The prayer for HANA is hidden in the seed. The seed grows into a flower that looks like the balloon that carried it from THE PLACE OF FREEDOM - puffed up and full of free air.

The dream of HANA begins to grow in the beauty of this flower. It waits to dispense the miracle designed by The Creator Himself. A miracle of LOVE, a miracle of ONE, waits to be enthroned in the heart of one who LOVES.

Young Ju, a little girl born into this hardened place
of no hopes or dreams, is drawn to walk where she
should not be, but she feels lead to be there.
You see, Young Ju has a secret. Jesus is in her heart,
whose name makes all things possible.
When she sees a flower growing where
no flowers or dreams should grow, she knows
that it is destined for her.
She runs to pick the flower and her heart
is filled with HOPE for HANA.
FAITH for HANA. LOVE for HANA.
Plucking the flower, she begins to walk home.
Little does she know that the DREAM for HANA
will take her on a long, hard journey.

The DREAM for HANA sends Young Ju through
THE PLACE WHERE DREAMS DIE.
She gives HOPE to those who want to leave
this place and cross The Freedom Bridge.

But, there are those who try to *BREAK* their HOPE for HANA.

She carries the DREAM for HANA to those who want to receive FAITH in The Creator of HANA.

But, there are those who try to *SHATTER*
their FAITH for HANA.

She carries LOVE to those who want HANA.

But, there are those who try to *TEAR APART*
their LOVE for HANA.

There are those who try to *DESTROY* Young Ju, whose heart is enthroned with the dream for HANA.

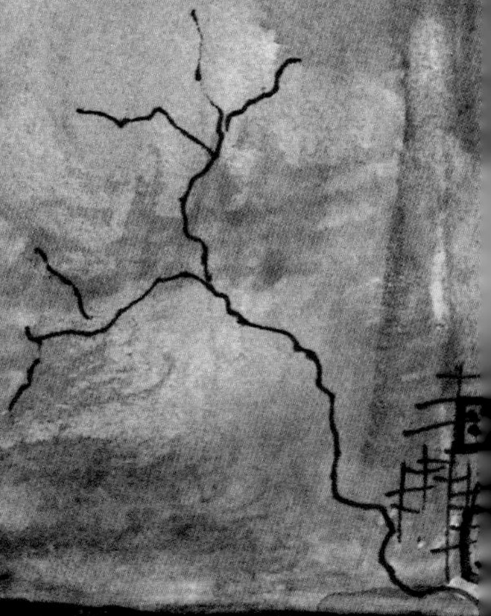

One day, there is a great gathering
of people, traveling from near and far.
They are forced to see the
destruction of others.
Inside their hard hearts marches hate -
HATE to stomp out the DREAM, HANA.

FEAR.
FEAR embraces DOUBT.
DOUBT turns to DESPAIR.
DESPAIR inflicts PAIN.
PAIN shadows HATE.
HATE invites DARKNESS.
FEAR makes DARK HEARTS HARD.
FEAR tries to put out the
LIGHT of LOVE.

But, the CREATORS LOVE casts out ALL *FEAR*.

LOVE.

In front of all of these people,
the LOVE for HANA
causes Young Ju to
shield the life of another
with her own.

Her act of LOVE is so incredible to see,
LOVE seems to fall on the
gathering crowd
of people, like
a soft rain.

The DREAM for HANA rises from the hardened ground. Their hearts are opened to LOVE.

And LOVE for HANA becomes their DREAM and their MISSION.

When Sung and the other children who released the balloons from THE PLACE OF FREEDOM, hear about the incredible act of LOVE, they run to The Freedom Bridge.

The great gathering of people on the other side of The Freedom Bridge follow Young Ju, with the DREAM for HANA in their hearts and the FREEDOM filled flowers in their hands. Together they start to tear down the fence that created *THE UGLIEST PLACE IN THE WORLD.*

Sung and Young Ju begin to cross
The Freedom Bridge.
When Sung sees Young Ju and the other
dreamers carrying puffed up purple flowers
across The Freedom Bridge,
she stops in her tracks.
"Can it be? Is my hope, my prayer, and my
impossible dream for one country, HANA, really
coming true? Did my seed for HANA
take root and grow?"
Young Ju stops the procession of people on their
way to freedom as she stands before Sung.
She can see the DREAM for HANA
is pouring out of her new found friend.
Reaching for Sung's hand, Young Ju places the
dream-filled flower in her palm. "Is this really
possible?" Sung whispers with tears in her eyes.
Young Ju holds Sung's hands in her own and
replies, "With Jesus, ALL things are possible!"

Together,
they hold the DREAM for HANA
and thank The Creator for this
DREAM that will NEVER *DIE*.

It is at this moment,
THE UGLIEST PLACE IN THE WORLD
ceases to exist, and
THE PLACE WHERE DREAMS DIE
begins to be tranformed by LOVE.

It is then united as ONE with
THE PLACE OF FREEDOM -
creating HANA.

All of the people are set FREE
to LOVE,
to DREAM,
to become,

HANA

And that's how HANA
crossed The Freedom Bridge
and became true.

. . .

HANA Crosses The Freedom Bridge
is dedicated:

- to the 130,000 (plus), men, women and CHILDREN who are currently imprisioned in the North Korean "Gulag" prison camps.

- to the millions of North Korean citizens who have lost their lives at the hands of their own Government.

- and to the people of Korea and the world who pray and believe that Korea will become ONE FREE NATION.

. . .

Sally Jo Messersmith and Krystyna Speaks generously donate from the proceeds of this book to help support North Korean CHILDREN who have escaped North Korea.

. . .

Glossary

and the big hard question

HANA - means ONE in Korean. We use it to represent one, united Korea.

The Freedom Bridge - a bridge located in the DMZ that stands as a symbol of hope that the divided nation will become one, free nation again.

THE UGLIEST PLACE IN THE WORLD - refers to the Demilitarized Zone, or the DMZ. It is a strip of land running across the Korean Peninsula at the 38th parallel. It was built to separate North Korea and South Korea.

THE PLACE OF FREEDOM - refers to South Korea.

THE PLACE WHERE DREAMS DIE - refers to North Korea.

The purple flower - is a Korean flower called a Doraji. All of the petals unite as one, similar to the shape of a balloon. In this story, the flower represents the dream for HANA.

The Colorful Fence - the fence running along the South Korean side of the DMZ is covered in colorful ribbons that people have written their hopes, dreams and prayers. Prayers for HANA. . . .

Why was Young Ju in prison and going to be executed?

This book doesn't begin to tell the full story of the inhumane acts that go on in North Korea. Individuals and entire generations of families are imprisioned for expressing thoughts of freedom, religion, or even learning about other ideas and cultures. Millions of North Koreans have been killed by their own government by starvation, murder, and public executions.

The background for this particular part of the story comes from an incident where Kim Jung Un publicly executed 80 citizens in a public arena, forcing thousands of people to watch. And I thought, what if one person had stood up and tried to protect someone from getting shot? Would it bring others to stand up and say "no more"? Would their courage and their love change the heart of a broken nation? . . .

For more symbolism, discussions and activities to go along with this book, please visit - www.HANA-OneFreeKorea.com - HANA Crosses The Freedom Bridge

About the Author

Sally Jo Messersmith lives in Michigan, and her heart is for Korea. Her cousin, Zola Payne, was a missionary in Korea when it was still one nation. Zola's letters about the Korean people inspired Sally Jo to pray for North Korea to be transformed by love, and that the divided nation would become ONE again.

Sally Jo wrote her first book, *AWAKEN HANA*, in 2015. *AWAKEN HANA* is a more in depth story about the underground railroad in North Korea, and is the "big sister book" to *HANA Crosses The Freedom Bridge.*

Sally Jo was able to travel to South Korea in 2016 and meet with the Korean *Voice Of The Martyrs,* who regularly send balloons, with Bibles and messages of hope, across the DMZ and into North Korea. Their dedication, faith, and courage inspired Sally Jo to write the childrens book *HANA Crosses the Freedom Bridge.*

Sally Jo hopes that this book will help to educate young people about the inhumane acts that the North Korean people have to face, and that they would be inspired to join her in praying for the divided nation to be healed by love and become HANA.

. . .

Thank you to Krystyna Speaks (Bobina Doodle) for her inspiring illustrations that express the vision of HANA, which will help many to believe for the impossible.

Thank you to Dorethea Abate for her guidance in formalizing the ideas in the book, editing and keeping it true to the vision of HANA.

And a special thanks to Young Ju, Julie, Jerry, Jason, Zuzu, Sully, and our other loved ones who have helped and supported us on our journey of HANA.

. . .

HANA

Crosses The Freedom Bridge

ISBN: 978-0-6921-9719-6 (hc)
Hard Cover (HANA-OneFreeKorea - Sally Jo Messersmith)

Library of Congress Control Number: 2018910260

Proudly Printed In The
USA

www.HANA-OneFreeKorea.com